Chromosome 23

John J. Duffy

John J. Duffy

Published in the United States

ISBN-13: 978-1490933894
ISBN-10: 1490933891

ABOUT THE COVER

A painting entitled
"The Mandarin Woman"

Poem
"The Love of An Artist
by
Nguyen Cao Nguyen)

The woman is a mosaic of shells.
She is beautiful beyond compare,
Dressed in a Mandarin costume of old,
Painted by Nguyen Cao Nguyen.

The model is his lovely young wife.
Love shows in the work of the artist.
Nothing makes a masterpiece as viewed,
As full of beauty as a lover in love.

Soon the war would separate them.
Children replaced the man at home.
The love would encompass a family.
This egg shell mosaic would be forever.

TABLE OF CONTENTS

INTRODUCTION
 A Poet and a Poem
 Power in Ink
 A Poem about Poems

CHROMOSOME 23
 A Simple Challenge
 The 23d Chromosome
 They Own the Egg
 The Delivery System
 The Scent of Woman
 Good to be Woman
 Scream
 Men, Enjoy!
 Lucy, the First Biped
 The "XX" Design
 The "XY" Design
 I Now Understand Woman
 The Future of Life

Table of Contents [cont.]

CHROMOSOME 23, LYRICS TO A MUSICAL
  The Big Bang (voice over introduction)
SONGS
  Chromosome of Love
  Hormone of Love
  Love Mix
  Love's Curves
  Love of Her
  Love of Him
  Loving Fun
  Goddess of Love
  We Need Love
  Love Hunt
  Love Call
  Love Signals
  Apple of Love
  Love Siren
  Orbit of Love
  My Love
  Love's Proposal
  Love March
  Belly of Love
  Love Seed
  Love's Fruit
  Gift of Love
  Love Story

Table of Contents [cont.]

THE BRAIN:
  Headspace: An Introduction
  Wants
  Now
  Fair/Unfair
  Trial and Error
  Judgment
  Logic
  Praise and Recognition
  Consciousness
  Memory
  Sleep
  Process
  Fear
  Flight or Fight
  Panic Understood
  Fear Overcome
  Don't Panic
  Neuroplasticity
  Neuroimaging
  Process Relations
  Real Mutations
  Libido
  It is Called Love
  The Love Factory
  The Brain House
  Brain Force
  We Begin With DNA
  The New Brain
  The Inner Universe
  Brain Reading 101

John J. Duffy

FOREWORD

Chromosome 23 is a story about you.

It is a story about me and all the rest of us. It delves into the "XX" and the "XY" chromosome. This is the female and the male chromosome.

"I never understand women." We've heard that before. This endeavor is the key to understanding women and the men they need. Women own and design the egg, all else follows.

Read "The Chromosome Dozen" and enlightenment is yours. Take a lyrical journey with words to the musical: "Chromosome 23".

Last, journey into the brain, your most important tool and vision how it functions. This journey is just beginning, read "Inner Universe", the most important discovery of anatomy.

John J. Duffy
Soldier, Businessman and Poet

John J. Duffy

INTRODUCTION

John J. Duffy

A Poet and a Poem

A poem is very personal,
And yet it is universal,
A sharing of oneself,
With those who will read a poem.

Power In Ink

A poem is not all trees and bees,
It is a bit more than a weak rhythm.
It is a source of inner expression
That you control with your scribbling.

Within the realm of the poet,
You can turn and twist words,
To evoke laughter, tears and fear.
It is words that bring forth emotion.

You can describe a woman as desirable.
You can provoke action from inaction.
You can make an idea come alive.
You can mourn for a friend now gone.

The tool kit of a poet is limitless.
One little thought can spark a pen.
Words develop thoughts to explore.
Thinking cements idea's which cause change.

The words: Liberty or death!
The words: I have a dream.
The words: One step for mankind.
All evoke pictures in the reader's mind.

These pictures germinate into action;
Soldiers march off to war because of words,
Equal rights imposed as the law of the land,
Thousands working in convert toward one goal.

Be the one to pick up the pen.
Be the one to write the words.
Be the one to scribble a poem,
Of love, of laughter, of drama, et cetera.

Etcetera means anything is possible,
When you write a poem conceived in mind.
Your mind is powerful; exercise and create
A poem for man, life or mankind.

A Poem About Poems

A poem is not like anything else;
It is a journey into man's soul,
It is an intimate glimpse into a mind,
It is a process of creation from within.

In a poem, one can tell a story,
One can evoke emotion and tears,
One can solve a problem by writing,
One can develop unique insights.

A piece of paper and a pen
Begin the journey of a poem,
Which may last as long as the ages,
Or be forgotten as soon as tomorrow.

Writing poetry is not at all difficult,
Anyone can have an idea and write
About a vision, a dream, a love.
It can be sad or it may be humorous.

A poem is a gem which can shine bright.
It can be carved into granite.
It can be transcribed onto bronze.
It can inspire generations to come.

CHROMOSOME 23

John J. Duffy

A Simple Challenge
(Chromosome 23)

The project came into my head.
One little poem, a lark in endeavor.
Can I write a poem on "XX" and "XY"?
That will be tricky, I like the challenge.

Well, I need to make it a trilogy.
It is not complete – I can see that.
Two more poems will do the trick.
I'm beginning to get the hang of this.

The trilogy is good but the story is not done.
There is more to life than three poems.
I'll write a bit more and figure it out.
This is beginning to get interesting.

Oh my God, I've discovered the truth.
It's "Scream" for me and it is real.
The horror of the discovery moves me forward.
I'll reconcile, adapt and get beyond the trauma.

A dozen poems concluded, what a task.
I now understand women as never before.
I have new knowledge, new power, new compassion.
Life is evolved evolvability: required for mankind.

The 23d Chromosome
(XX {female} or XY (male))

Will the baby be a male or a female?
The helix of life is a double strand,
Twenty three matched pairs with one exception,
The twenty third chromosome is unique.

It is composed of a double "XX",
Or it can be an "X" and a "Y".
The "XY" is the male of the mammals.
The "XX" is the female of the species.

The "X" has ten hundred and ninety genes.
A female "XX" has twenty one hundred eighty genes.
A male "Y" chromosome has seventy eight genes,
An "XY" male is eleven hundred sixty eight genes.

A male's donation to sexuality is undiluted.
A female is a combine of her genes
Mixed with traces of all her female lineage.
Male traits in offspring appear more pronounced.

Although a child may look like the father,
It is more strongly influenced by the mother.
A combine of genes in females is about equal,
In boys, it is twelve female genes to each male gene.

A girl is much more the child of her parents
Than a boy who really is his mother's son.
In the procreation process, it is the female,
Who passes more intellect, beauty and ability.

They Own The Egg

Women have ownership of the egg.
It is theirs and always has been.
The male implants his sperm.
Mostly at the invitation of the female.

It is a design of the millenniums;
Modified, changed and improved.
From hunched "Lucy" to the smiling "Mona Lisa",
It is the woman's creation.

The egg of life delivers:
A male developed with fewer genes,
A male with specialized traits,
A male designed to be useful.

This clever egg even allows
The offspring to look like the Dad,
While being intelligent, able
And beautiful like the mother.

The design develops aggressive males
And a passive female with beauty,
That bears and rears the children.
Women know, a male can be replaced.

Addendum:
What are you men smiling at?
You have been scammed in life.
You may be bigger and stronger,
In essence, you are the delivery system.

The Delivery System

You display like a peacock.
The mirror returns your love.
How can women resist you.
You are young and strong?

That is the "chorus" of young males.
They exude aggressive confidence.
They flex their muscles and strut.
They smile at all the young ladies.

The women have their choice.
The males are infinitely attracted
To the curves of enchanting women.
To the movement of the female.

The trap has been baited and set:
The soft voice, demure eyes,
The hold me and protect me look.
They all need our shoulder and love.

Social mores change and develop.
The cycle of love remains in place.
How can one overcome nature?
"I must have a mate to mate with!"

The Scent of Woman

How do you compare a male and a female?
The female starts with many more genes.
Her development is faster, mature at eighteen,
The male brain linkage is complete at twenty four.

Women test better and are more verbally skilled.
When the hormones testosterone and estrogen
Enter the youthful system after puberty,
The change becomes significantly identifiable.

The women develop breasts and inviting curves.
Their bottoms fill out as do their lips.
Their voices are softer and their eyes larger.
The boys begin to develop facial hair and muscle.

The scent of woman attracts and males pursue.
The woman selects her mate and is unique:
Only the women can reproduce and feed offspring.
This requires home making and child rearing.

The male must provide and sustain a family.
He must work and defend his family.
His tasks oftentimes incur risks to life and limb.
This the woman knows, she needs a reliable male.

Good To Be A Woman

A girl needs to be attractive.
That is the nature of mating.
Man needs to desire woman
Before the ritual can begin.

Men look at our breasts and buns.
They love long legs and flowing hair,
A smile that captivates and lips in bloom.
I have curves and they focus men.

You would think that should be enough.
But, I use lipstick and eye shadow,
A little perfume and fingernail polish,
To add a touch of allure to my presence.

A girl needs to be noticed to attract.
My high heels stand me above the rest,
My walking is curves in motion to delight,
Either front or back, the view is appealing.

My look is demure and a little shy.
My smile can encourage a little more.
My voice is soft, a melody to males.
Oh, it's good to be a woman and attractive.

Scream

The pleasure and the joy of woman,
Nothing compares to mating.
It is both a pleasure and a release.
And a fulfillment of life's destiny.

A woman offers pleasure with a kiss,
The pleasure of anticipation of more.
The curves and the softness entice.
The pleasure to come becomes focus.

Enticement, anticipation and delight,
All in the arms of a sweet soft woman.
There is nothing more to life's flow
Than binding in pleasure with a woman.

This is the perception of the male.
This is the belief of the male.
This is the male's great gift to woman.
Oh glory, males are magnificent!

Reality, oh brutal reality is truth.
Your seed is delivered and implanted.
With your last delivery, you are done.
Your usefulness to mankind is obsolete.

Men, Enjoy!

Men are the supporting actors.
The star in the show of life
Is and always has been woman.
She owns and programs the egg of life.

You are her product, she produced you.
You can contribute and perform.
You first and foremost deliver the seed.
You must desire and pursue woman.

You support the effort with work.
You protect the family with courage.
You can also pass on your knowledge,
Your brain is yours, this you own.

Enjoy the curves of woman and love's rapture.
Enjoy the challenges that have been presented.
Enjoy your role as a supporting actor,
Encourage women and assist them.

In reality, you work best as a team,
Two people in process to better mankind.
Yours is a noble endeavor.
Look around and see mankind, your creation.

Lucy, The First Biped

"You're telling me "Lucy" stood upright?"
The bones dug-up tell the story.
She was a biped, the first of her kind.
She changed the story of mankind.

The climate changed, the rains stopped.
Over decades, the jungle became less
And food became less and fought over.
This was an escape from hunger.

In a group they would move to seek
A new domain with food and shelter.
The journey would be long and dangerous.
A biped could move faster on the open plains.

Lions, hyenas and alligators would attack.
A two legged person could run faster,
Rejoin the group as it foraged ever Eastward.
The group was a safe haven from danger.

Eventually, the coast was reached
And crustaceans would become diet,
Giving substance and protein to new man.
We are biped man, we cover the earth.

The "XX" Design

I must be attractive for mating.
I'll have a slender body of curves
With enticements both front and rear.
They will bounce as I walk and cause focus.

I need not be taller than my mate,
As he will protect and provide.
I'll also need the pleasure of mating
And their need be no limit on endurance.

I'll need extra body fat for survival.
Let the male be lean, he'll hunger quickly.
I'll live off my internal reserve of fat.
Yes, my breasts and bottom will round perfectly.

Procreation is the rule of the species survival.
My breasts will feed my offspring for years.
The children and I will bind my mate,
He'll need to return to fulfill his urge to protect.

I'll be verbally more capable than my mate.
With language, I'll be capable of persuasion.
I'll design full lips and a soft voice.
My eyes will be larger and view better closer.

This will be a dynamic attractive creature.
Woman as art form, beauty to be pursued.
God did not create woman, woman created woman.
"I designed the male too, designed to perform."

The "XY" Design

I need protection by man.
He must be bigger and stronger.
I need substance provided by man.
He must want to work and be able.

His body fat need be less than mine,
As he will hunt and provide substance.
When he becomes hungry, I'll still be full.
When he returns from the hunt, I'll be hungry.

He must desire my slender body.
My curves must attract him to me.
His desire must be observable
So I'll know when to proceed.

He must be capable of delivering his seed
And he must want to procreate.
I must devise a method to bind him,
So that he will provide substance to offspring.

His physic and masculinity must attract me.
He must be capable of providing sexual joy.
But he should be limited of sexual endurance.
It is me he must satisfy, no one else.

I'll provide a beard so I can see him afar.
As a male, he could be a mate or a threat.
His eyes should see distance for hunting.
Less verbal skills, he need not talk too much.

One last thing, he must be aggressive.
I need to see him in performance
Thus I can weed out the weaker pretenders.
Yes, all men are to be easily replaced.

I Now Understand Woman

Why another poem in this chromosome story?
Because I have discovered the answer,
The answer to understanding women.
It is simple once discovered as all things are.

If you know the design concept of Chromosome 23,
You will understand the methods of women.
You comprehend the dynamics of life.
You now know the algorithm of mankind.

The appeal and need to mate and procreate
Are inherent in the survival and improvement.
The drive evolves into a better "You" design.
You are more intelligent, attractive and stronger.

We need to adapt to survive as a species.
You live, make love, have children and enjoy.
This is within the design of chromosome 23.
Women are more clever than they look, they design.

Once you understand the dynamics of life,
All else falls into place, nothing else distracts.
Woman designed and evolution continues.
Enjoy woman. She designed you for the task.

The Future of Life

You are a creature.
I am a creature.
We have evolved in time,
From beginning to now.

Change is inherent.
We must all adapt.
Without adaptation,
We shall all perish.

This is the story of life.
We live, we evolve, we adapt.
We become smarter, faster, stronger.
We surpass our rivals.

The number of species
Is less that have evolved,
Than the number that are extinct.
Life form is a struggle.

The river of life is complex.
We are still evolving.
The future of all life
Is to evolve <u>evolvability</u>.

John J. Duffy

CHROMOSOME 23
LYRICS TO A MUSICAL

John J. Duffy

SONGS

A poem is a song without a chorus.

I've taken the Chromosome 23 Dozen" poems and created one VoiceOver Introduction plus twenty-three songs that compose the lyrics to a musical about you and me and all of us. It's about the soup mix that forms our helix of life. It's about boys, girls, love, marriage, and babies. All we need is music and little things like costumes, props, a theatre and, of course, an audience.

The Big Bang
(Voice-Over c23 Introduction)

The "Big Bang" happened fourteen billion years ago.
The universe, galaxies and stars began.
When a star collapses, it is a super-nova.
From a super-nova: our sun and the earth.

Five billion years ago, the earth was born.
Two billion years ago, life form began.
Human kind began two hundred million years ago.
We came from stardust, fire and energy.

We survived with great difficulty.
Once there were but a few dozen of us.
With grit and endeavor, we multiplied,
Gathering our food and then hunting our food.

When the hunting would no longer provide,
We innovated and began to grow our food.
That was a mere ten thousand years ago,
A blink of time in the life of the universe.

We ground our grain in the water powered wind mills.
We harnessed horse and domesticated animals.
Coal fueled our machines as well as petroleum.
We are now developing wind and solar as energy sources.

Seven billion of mankind and we dominate.
Eighty thousand species vanished, twenty thousand survive.
Mankind is the driving force of planet "Earth",
All developed in the womb of woman, in the helix of life.

Chromosome of Love
(The 23d Chromosome)
(c23 song)

I'll sing a song of life.
I'll sing of the beginning.
I'll sing of you and me.
I'll sing about the helix of life.

The helix of life is the chromosomes,
Twenty three pairs will bind.
The male and female differ,
One is "XY", the other "XX".

The "XX" female selects randomly.
Near half and half from each mate.
Eleven hundred genes each
Are pruned to combine as life.

The "XY" male is less complex:
It combines seventy-eight genes,
The male partners contribution
With eleven hundred of the female.

This is the woman's task to begin,
The traits and quirks we call us.
This is the design of millenniums,
A design created by woman.

Short, tall, blue eyes or brown,
With strength and sexuality,
Life is what we have – it is gifted,
By woman with man enjoining her.
<u>Chorus</u>
I'll sing a song of life.
I'll sing of the beginning.
I'll sing of you and me.
I'll sing about the helix of life.

Hormone of Love
(c23 song)

All little girls grow up
And will become women,
With curves and shape,
With buns and busts.

The chemicals of life
Flow and evoke change.
Estrogen is woman's choice,
That does the trick for her.

This hormone changes her
Into a lovely creatures of desire.
She morphs from no interest
To focusing on the boys.

It's about the boys in life.
It's about being attractive.
It's about interacting with them.
It's about young girls needing boys.

They should take notice of me.
I need to be as pretty as I can be.
I'll groom and comb my hair,
A little lipstick and I'm ready boys.

<u>Chorus</u>
It's about the boys in life.
It's about being attractive.
It's about interacting with them.
It's about young girls and boys.

Love Mix
(c23 song)

Little boys will grow tall.
Hormones cause change in them,
Testosterone is the juice of man.
They will soon morph into men.

The girls once uninteresting
Now become objects of desire.
A boy needs to date a girl.
A boy needs a girl in his life.

The muscles firm and expand.
The boy can even shave his face.
He grooms and combs his hair,
Prancing for mirror and girls.

Oh, it's the girls I attract.
Oh, it's the girls that notice.
I'm strong and full of life.
I'm the young man for girls.

So, the dance of life begins:
Boy meets girl, dance with me,
Hold my hand and give me a kiss.
I'm in love with a sweet girl.

<u>Chorus</u>
Oh, it's the girls I attract.
Oh, it's the girls that notice.
I'm full of life and strong.
I'm the young man for girls.

Love's Curves
(c23 song)

Give me a girl with breasts and buns.
Give me a girl with all the form.
Give me something to focus my eyes upon.
Give me a girl that will be mine to love.

The boys all "ogle" the girls with curves.
The boys look at the breasts and buns.
They check us out and view it all,
Like they have never seen a girl before.

I need to see a girl in motion.
I need to see the whole package.
I need to see the bounce in her form.
I need a girl that keeps me focused.

I need to be a girl with all of the curves.
I need to be a girl with all of the form.
I need the tributes of my sex to show
If I expect to catch a boy that will be mine.
<u>Chorus</u>
Give me a girl with breasts and buns.
Give me a girl with all the form.
Give me something to focus my eyes upon.
Give me a girl that will be mine to love.

Chromosome 23

Love of Her
(c23 song)

Oh woman, you are a temptation.
Oh woman, you are desirable.
Oh woman, you are delectable.
Oh woman, where art thou?

I need a woman in my life.
Life is incomplete without her.
I need a woman to frolic with.
I need a woman to make love to.

My life is a lonely journey,
Until I find the woman for me.
Then, I'll have my hands full
Of woman and all the rest.

Let me hold her hand at first,
Soon I'll kiss as we acquaint.
It is woman I need for more
And more I need to do with woman.

I'll seek her out all over.
I'll find her where so ever she is.
I'll strut my stuff for woman.
I'll show her that I am the one.

<u>Chorus</u>
Oh woman, you are a temptation.
Oh woman, you are desirable.
Oh woman, you are delectable.
Oh woman, where art thou?

Love of Him
(c23 song)

Oh my man, I am attracted to you.
Oh my man, I need you to want me.
Oh my man, I need you to love me.
Oh my man, I need you to find me soon.

I am not complete without man.
I need a man to hold me tight
And to delight me with his love.
I need a man to be my mate.

My life is filled with desire for you.
I dream of you each and every night.
I dream of man to join with me.
I dream of man and all the rest.

Whether he is short or tall,
I'll know him when I see him.
He'll be the one to protect me.
He'll be the one to cherish me.

He will see, I am at my best.
I'm as shapely as any can be.
My eyes will talk, my voice is soft,
He'll feel the flame when he finds me.

<u>Chorus</u>
Oh my man, I am attracted to you.
Oh my man, I need you to want me.
Oh my man, I need you to love me.
Oh my man, I need you to find me soon.

Loving Fun
(c23 song)

Girls and boys just want to have fun.
We like the beat of the music we love.
We like to dance and show off in time.
We want to be seen. We want to be loved.

Listen to the beat! Listen to the music!
It brings you around, it makes you alive.
Show me a girl bumping and grinding,
I'll show you a boy falling in love with her.

Girls and boys get together for fun,
To dance, to hug, to hold each other in joy.
It is the way it has always been, no new thing.
It is fun, we are young, a kiss is what we want.

So let it be. Let us dance. Let us kiss for love.
We'll hold, we'll touch, we'll find love's rhythm.
It is the way of youth. It is the way I am.
I'm hot. I'm sexy. I need someone to love.
<u>Chorus</u>
So let it be. Let us dance. Let us kiss for love.
We'll hold, we'll touch, we'll find love's rhythm.
It is the way of youth. It is the way I am.
I'm hot. I'm sexy. I need someone to love.

Goddess of Love
(c23 song)

Girl, you have no idea what you do to men.
Your curves and movement are enchantment.
Your breasts are creations of the Gods.
Your legs are long and beauty in motion.

I look into your dark brown eyes
And I see the compassion of a woman.
When you smile, I am captivated.
Your voice is melody to my ears.

Girl, when you walk, all eyes view you.
It is a movement synchronized for viewing.
I'm in love, all men are in love with you.
You are beauty meant to captivate and capture.

I am but a man, mortal in all respects.
You have power over me like no other.
I am in your circle like so many others.
Because you are a Goddess and I am man.

Chorus
I am but a man, mortal in all respects.
You have power over me like no other.
I am in your circle like so many others.
Because you are a Goddess and I am man.

We Need Love
(c23 song)

We need each other to hold.
We need each other to frolic.
We need each other to love.
We need each other to mate.

This is the truth of love.
This is the truth of life.
This is the truth of mankind.
The truth, we need each other.

We seek each other out in time.
We seek the bind that is fine.
We seek the love that is wine.
We seek another that will be mine.

It is romance and a dance.
It is kissing and not letting go.
It is passion and love nesting.
It is our need to hold each other.

Chorus
We seek each other out in time.
We seek the bind that is fine.
We seek to love that is wine.
We seek another that will be mine.

Chromosome 23

Love Hunt
(c23 song)

The flow of life is in your genes.
The flow of life is in your desire.
The flow of life is in your mating
With woman who needs your love.

You display like a peacock.
The mirror returns your love.
How can women resist you,
You are strong and youthful?

You flex your muscles and strut.
You exude aggressive confidence.
You smile at all the young ladies,
Knowing one will smile back at you.

It is good to be a man in life.
You have so many chances at love.
The women are many and you are one,
Ready to pleasure them with love's flame.

This is your belief, this is your hope,
That women will find you desirable,
That women will take you in their arms,
That women will open herself to you.

<u>Chorus</u>
The flow of life is in your genes.
The flow of life is in your desire.
The flow of life is in your mating
With woman who needs your love.

Love Call
(c23 song)

I sing a song of life.
I sing a song of love.
I sing a song of renewal.
I sing a song about you.

You are the creation of woman.
She designs and owns the egg.
We are all loves final tally,
You, me, the world's peoples.

It is truly marvelous,
The joy of sexual encounter.
It is the combination of us.
It is joy and creation.

When she smiles at you,
Perk up and take notice.
This may be your moment,
To encounter and triumph.

The joys of woman are yours,
The curves, the softness, the sight.
Sweet kisses lead to paradise,
Enraptured delight like no other.
Chorus
It is truly marvelous,
The joy of sexual encounter.
It is the combination of us.
It is joy of creation.

Love Signals
(c23 song)

Return my smile with a smile.
Tell me with your eyes to continue.
Show me with a nod that you listen.
Let me begin this ritual of love.

These signals are part of the process
Of getting to know each the other.
The signals are in a smile, your eyes,
In the way that you lead me on.

Forward we move until in our time
We begin displaying our interest;
Walking together, touching as we need,
Showing affection as love blossoms.

This is the time of knowing each other.
This is the time of intimacy and love.
This is the time we think beyond pleasure.
This is a time we think of life entwined.

<u>Chorus</u>
Return my smile with a smile.
Tell me your eyes to continue.
Show me with a nod that you listen.
Let me begin this ritual of love.

Apple of Love
(c23 song)

I bit the apple of love.
I swallowed the sweet fruit.
I must have this creature.
She must be mine to delight.

She smiles at me in turn.
My heart beat rages within.
I feel the flames of love.
I feel the heat of passion.

A caress from her is rapture.
And a kiss has me in paradise.
It is her and only her for me.
I love this woman, I'm in love.

I dream of a night with her.
I cannot sleep for excitement.
I awake and I think of her.
She must be mine, I must have her.

Chorus
I bit the apple of love.
I swallowed the sweet fruit.
I must have this creature.
She must be mine to delight.

Love Siren
(c23 song)

I am woman and woman is me.
I attract, I enchant and I provide.
No one else can replace me.
I am woman and woman is me.

Check me out, view my curves.
I'll smile at you if you please me.
Watch me walk, see me in motion.
Can you take your eyes off of me?

My eyes can be demure or bold.
Look at me! Can you look away?
I'll hold you with my eyes on you,
Or I'll turn away and leave you be.

My lips entice, red and full of love.
I need to smile before there is more.
I'm designed to attract, slim in waist.
Breasts full and my bottom shapely.

Yes, I know, your eyes focus on me.
It is meant to be, woman is me
And you are man – designed by woman,
Designed to cherish, mate and love.
Chorus
I am woman and woman is me.
I attract, I enchant, I provide.
No one else can replace me.
I am woman and woman is me.

John J. Duffy

Orbit of Love
(c23 song)

We kiss, we caress, we hold,
This is not enough for us.
More we need, more we'll have,
We begin our dance of love.

We dance to the music,
Our hearts beat out the rhythm
To a crescendo of rapture,
To a crescendo of love.

This dance is our life form.
This binding is our pleasure.
The rapture is love's reward,
With delight like no other.

This is the passion of lover's.
This is the fire of binding.
This is the explosion of galaxies,
Which create the orbit of life.
<u>Chorus</u>
We dance to the music,
Our hearts beat out the rhythm
To a crescendo of rapture,
To a crescendo of love.

My Love
(c23 song)

(Her name), it is only you my love
That I will commit my love to.
You are my desire, you are my future,
You are my hope for happiness.

I need you beyond all others.
I want you to be my companion
I want you to be my life mate.
I want you to commit to marriage.

I will be your partner in all.
I will love you as much as life.
I will respect and treasure you.
I will honor you with my true love.

Together, we will make the journey.
We will enjoy our life entwined.
We will blossom as only a couple can.
I beg you for your hand in marriage.

Take this ring and wear it true.
We'll seal it with a kiss of love.
Let the world know of our love.
Let all celebrate our happiness.
<u>Chorus</u>
Together, we will make the journey.
We will enjoy our life entwined.
We will blossom only as a couple can.
I beg you for your hand in marriage.

Love's Proposal
(c23 song)

My love proposed to me.
We are going to be married.
Come see my diamond ring.
It is romance and love for me.

It will be a celebration,
A wedding to remember.
My gown will be in white.
He'll be handsome in tuxedo.

We'll party with friends and family,
We'll wine and dine all night long.
This marriage will bind us
And proclaim our love to all.

I'll toss my bouquet to the girls,
One of you will be the next to marry.
I'll remove my garter and present
To a husband that will be mine.

There will be treats and champagne.
There will be party favors and music.
There will be feasting and drinking.
There will be dancing and fireworks.
Chorus
My love proposed to me.
We are going to be married.
Come see my diamond ring.
It is romance and love for me.

Love March
(c23 song)

We sing of passion.
We sing of heat.
We sing of love.
The flame burns bright.

Love and love's fire,
We delight in its pleasure,
But there is more to life
Than the joy of romance.

We must choose our mate.
We must bind in harmony.
We must endeavor to relate
Beyond the heat and fire.

This is the commitment.
This indeed is love of two.
I will commit myself to thee
In a marriage for eternity.

The attraction, desire and the fire,
All are part of this dance of love.
We must now begin the journey,
Hand in hand, married for life.
<u>Chorus</u>
This is the commitment.
This indeed is love of two.
I will commit myself to thee
In a marriage for eternity.

Belly of Love
(c23 song)

I sing about the needs of woman.
I sing about the needs of life.
I sing about the needs of mankind.
I sing about you loving me.

The dance of selection is done.
You are the one I've chosen.
You are the one I give myself to.
You are the one to fill my belly.

There is more to life than pleasure.
You are the one that will make that be.
You are the one to implant in me:
The seed of life, the seed of thee.

For I have a need that is great,
I must have children in life
To bear and love as my own.
You and I must provide for a life.
Chorus
I sing about the needs of woman.
I sing about the needs of life.
I sing about the needs of mankind.
I sing about you loving me.

Love Seed
(c23 song)

I am man, I am strong.
I am man, I am smart.
I am man, I am daring.
I am man, I spread my seed.

I mate with my love of life.
I enjoy the pleasure of love.
I cherish and hold my wife.
I plant my seed hoping for life.

This, a new life is my doing.
I am the one to implant in woman.
I am the one to provide for family.
I am man, needed by woman.

I do my work and endeavor
To provide as we must thrive.
I play my part in this cycle,
A strong man needed by woman.
<u>Chorus</u>
I am man, I am strong.
I am man, I am smart.
I am man, I am daring.
I am man, I spread my seed.

John J. Duffy

Love's Fruit
(c23 song)

I'm so excited I could burst.
I'll tell my man right away,
He'll be shocked, but we did it.
We did it, I am expectant.

A baby is growing inside of me.
I don't care if it's a boy or a girl,
I just want it to be a baby.
I want to be a caring mother.

The happening seems so strange,
To create another life within me.
I'll take care: no wine, no smoking,
I'll exercise and control myself.

This baby is everything to me.
This baby is a new life in me.
My husband will be thrilled.
He is a father soon to be "Papa".
<u>Chorus</u>
I'm so excited I could burst.
I'll tell my man right away,
He'll be shocked, but we did it.
We did it, I am expectant.

Gift of Love
(c23 song)

A baby is inside of me.
He is growing each and every day.
He'll be big, healthy and strong,
Or maybe he will be a she.

If it's a girl, I'll dress her up,
She'll be pretty and eye catching.
I will have a girl in my life
And she'll grow up to be a wife.

Boy or girl, what do I care.
It is going to be a baby of mine.
It will be a new life to hold.
It will be a child to love.

Baby will grow, I'll feel it soon.
A kick inside if me to signal
All goes well in the belly of love,
All goes well with my baby.

It could be more than one.
It could be two or more.
That really would be a chore,
But two would be better than one.
<u>Chorus</u>
A baby is inside of me.
He is growing each and every day.
He'll be big, strong and healthy,
Or maybe he will be a she.

Love Story
(c23 song)

You want to know the stories end.
You want to know a boy or a girl.
You want to know happy ever after.
You want to know the rest of the story.

It is you and me in our day.
It is our children to be in time.
It is grand children and more.
It is endeavor and mankind.

It is the love and triumphs of life.
It is great joy and tragedy.
It is the rollercoaster of living,
The laughter and also the tears.

It is getting on in our pursuits.
It is our struggle and our success.
It is being part of the human race.
It is life; you, me and family.

The rest of the story is your story.
Sing your song about being happy.
Sing your song about your love in life.
Sing your song about mating and babies.
Chorus
You want to know the stories end.
You want to know a boy or a girl.
You want to know happy ever after.
You want to know the rest of the story.

THE BRAIN

YOUR MOST IMPORTANT TOOL

John J. Duffy

The Brain

This is a presentation of some of the functions which our brain performs.

The Latin subtitles refer to the particular areas within the brain where it is believed they occur.

Headspace: An Introduction
Cerebrum

This is the story of the brain.
It is a tool, nothing more, but nothing less.
Some tools are complex, some are easy.
The brain is both complex and simple.

It is a miracle of development.
It took tens of thousands of years,
To bring it into its current form,
And it is still developing.

It is intimidating to many,
But to others, it is a simple tool.
Each and every brain is different,
But each is yet similarly formed.

Read about the parts of the brain,
And then you will comprehend,
That this tool is your own, to control.
And it is the process that is paramount.

Wants
Striatum

The brain is programmed to want,
You and I want many things.
First, we want warmth and food—
As we exit the womb of woman.

The wants take us through infancy,
And we announce our wants loudly,
With a cry for attention and need:
This the method we have to survive.

And even when we can nourish,
Without the aid of others,
We still want and need assistance,
But, now we communicate our wants.

It is many years forward in time,
Before we can take care of our own wants,
But, then we still want other things:
To play, to work, to fulfill our needs.

The brain that dictates our wants,
It functions until the end,
The wants change as we mature:
But the brain still conjures wants.

Now
Limbic System

Into the world we arrive,
And we know not about clocks,
We have no inkling about time;
All we know, is now, or later.

This now demand is born with us,
It is part of our survival.
Without this timely demand,
Others would not know our need.

Even a baby knows it is hungry,
And it screams its wants out loud.
The want is an imperative need,
Now is when it wants its need.

In life's progress, we learn of time,
And the essence of being patient.
Some even learn, how to postpone,
The wants and the needs until later.

The ability to postpone one's wants,
From now until sometime later,
These are learned traits in the brain.
To have self discipline is control.

Fair/Unfair
Anterior Insula

As we grow from toddler,
Ever developing and growing,
To the beginning of adulthood,
We learn the rules of society.

Within the brains of all of us,
The reasoning looks out beyond,
And evokes our sense of fairness,
And of what we think is unfair.

These exchanges within our thoughts,
Confront us even when very young,
And many times we are frustrated,
When we believe, it is unfair.

Even as adults, we can discern,
That some things are fair or unfair.
The essence of man's judgments,
Are besieged with the fairness of all.

When we believe it is unfair,
We react in an opposing way.
These learned perceptions in the brain:
Are the essence of later judgments.

Trial and Error
Nucleus Accumbens

It is the way of mankind,
To try something and experiment,
Hoping this trial will develop,
And hoping we have got it right.

But in the trial and error thesis,
Often, we end up in error,
And in turn, we must incorporate;
This failure as part of learning.

Judgment
Anterior Cingulate

Each and every day we judge,
To do something or not to do it.
It is our nature to learn to decide,
What is right and what is not right.

These judgments take place within.
The brain is processing information.
The brain is designed to make decisions.
The brain is looking for the best answer.

This the brain we develop,
After we enter the world of light,
After we receive inputs from all around,
After we learn fair and unfair perception.

A decision made on our judgment,
Oftentimes is correct and safe.
But, on occasion, we get it wrong.
It is these judgments we learn from.

The judgment brain is but a tool,
Within the arsenal of our brain.
But, it is the one that dictates our fate.
It is the one we are responsible for.

Logic
Prefrontal Cortex

Within the structure of our brain,
Taking up the bulk of the room,
And not fully developed until late,
Resides the brain we call logic.

It is the slowest and longest growing,
Of the brain's many complex parts.
It involves the full essence of learning.
It is the reservoir of all knowledge.

This, the brain that supplies the input,
To the rest of the complex structure.
The wants and needs are screened –
Against the possibility of "doing".

Logic supplies the information,
And we make life's decisions.
Some are minor, some are major,
But we must decide what is right.

The slow development of logic,
It is itself very logical,
As decisions are life's future–
And we need time to get it right.

Praise and Recognition
Nucleus Accumbers

Our brain responds to stimuli,
In both the negative and the positive.
Failure and its repercussions
Invoke negative reaction in us.

But, we have a positive force within
That is motivated by encouragement.
It could be a little praise from others,
Or recognition by our peer group.

These positive inputs do stimulate.
They activate the intellect we have,
We feel the surge of endeavor,
The raindrops of human compassion.

This acknowledgment by others,
That our tasking is worthy,
That we are valued for our effort,
It is the light we seek at the tunnels end.

Consciousness
Amygdala

It is the essence of ourselves,
Each and every one of us is different,
Each and everyone of us is unique,
And yet we are all similar.

The evolutionary biology developed,
Extending our gene networks,
To encompass image and language,
Which allow vision and interaction.

We interact with each other,
And we interact with our environment.
This interaction is consciousness –
And our history is our unique self.

We are continually exposed to inputs,
Which modify our interactions,
And develop change and modification.
The basic self adapts and changes.

Consciousness evolves during our lifetimes,
But we are always who we are.
Mental patterns, conversation and image,
Are simply the conscious being.

Memory
Neocortex

The sensory organs gather inputs
That feed information to the brain,
Where interpretation is encoded,
And moved into storage we call memory.

This all takes place routinely,
Each and every day we gather,
Each and every day we analyze,
Each and everyday we store.

The value of human memory is great.
It is the history of our past deeds.
It is the predictor of future actions.
This large memory bank is man's triumph.

Sleep
Hippo Campus

Each and every day, we tire,
And sleep envelops our system.
This is so in the animal realm,
Sleep is part of a daily cycle.

No one knows the reason for sleep,
Speculation is all that we have.
But while we sleep each night,
Our brain processes information.

Often time, we rerun daily events,
And modify in sleep those happenings.
In essence, the brains system
Are reviewing and storing.

When we wake up each morning,
Our brain has been modified.
The information of sleep
Is now part of our logic brain.

When someone says to you:
"I'll sleep on the problem."
They are in reality hoping
The problem will solve in sleep.

Process
Cerebrum

Knowledge and intellect help,
But we must be able to integrate,
And we must be able to process,
Before we make our decisions.

The process is the key to the brain.
It unlocks the inner workings,
And gives coherent organization,
The opportunity to format adaptation.

If you get the process in place,
Even errors become leaning vehicles,
As process incorporates review –
And change in process is feasible.

Fear
Amygdala

A paralyzing mind-numbing daze,
That makes you want to be sick,
And to run at the same time:
That is the thing we call fear.

Fear increases exponentially.
The closer you get to your fear,
The greater the fear impacts,
And the more fearful you are.

You cannot focus on anything,
Except the thing you fear.
Fear makes the mind perceptive.
You function at peak efficiency.

Fear anticipates a danger.
Fear can become terror in turn.
And too much fear is paralyzing –
Until panic captures your reactions.

Fear is the response to threat,
Which anticipates reactions.
Fear must be controlled,
Or it will control you.

Flight or Fight
Amygdala

When danger is present,
And we perceive that threat;
We must quickly decide,
To take flight or fight.

This is a survival mode,
Which is inherent to life.
In time not so far distant,
Animals looked at us as a meal.

We had to flee from some,
Or we had to fight them off.
Some were slow, and we were fast,
Others faster, so we had to fight.

Times have changed for many,
And we no longer fear,
That an animal will eat us,
But other dangers are present.

When we see a new danger:
Say a bully, or a snake in the grass,
The decision is still the same,
Do we run or do we fight?

Panic Understood
Amygdala

We have all panicked at one time.
We have all lost that sense of control,
Whatever triggered the event, it panicked us.
This is a normal primitive survival reaction.

It could be an examination or a test,
Or we may be called upon to give a speech.
Our prefrontal cortex shuts down our norm,
We panic: fight or flight or freeze arrive.

How does one deal with this real panic?
Stop, pause, breath, relax and think:
"I am losing control of the situation,
My most basic instincts are dominant."

An examination or public speaking
Are not equivalent to a tiger in the bush.
You are not in danger, your brain tricked you.
Relax, breath, gain control – do not panic.

Now you are in control, you are normal.
Sounds simple, it is simple when understood.
Your brain is designed foremost for survival,
It will react to a threat instinctively.

Fear Overcome
Amygdala

Fear is motivating force
In the brain of man,
When our logic dictates,
This is too dangerous.

Most heed the warning:
The internal alarm,
They back out of danger,
Fearful of the endeavor.

There are few of us
Who will flirt with danger,
Testing the edge of the blade,
Enjoying danger's moment.

This dance of glory and death,
With only one prevailing,
Is the edge of life,
Where fear is overcome.

Don't Panic
Amygdala

Panic is a normal reaction to fear.
Our fear is a product of not knowing.
The unknown frightens all of us.
The "boogey man" is a bad person.

The person who handles stress best
Is the one who is most prepared.
He or she must be highly alert,
Trained in the aspects of stress control.

It is another form of problem solving
While being subjugated to stress
I'm talking about unknown events:
In military combat, a cockpit or sports.

Selection and training plus stamina
All help you control the "bad" situation,
Maintain control, don't ever lose control.
Think it out, work the problem to solution.

Focus and preparation are ingredients
That allow one to never lose control of oneself.
Be prepared, be ready, expect the unexpected.
Surprises are inherent, "don't panic" ever.

Neuroplasticity
Cerebrum

The brain is the best tool we have.
It controls our every action,
And plans our future moves,
In all the phases of our life.

Much like sand on a beach,
The brain retains our footprints,
The skills that we have learned,
The actions that we have taken.

The brain even retains the thoughts
That we have used in our plans,
And inputs from the outside world.
The brain is sculpted into one's "self."

The dogma of a brain in adulthood:
Fixed in form and in function –
It is not the way it is at all.
The brain can rewire and rezone.

It is neuroplasticity at its best,
Even thinking can change format.
The mind can change the brain.
The power of the brain is within us.

Neuroimaging
Cerebrum

The brain is our learning tool.
Each and every brain is optimized,
Even the timing is programmed.
The brain is structured to develop.

The brain utilizes mirror neurons,
Which simplify our learning process,
By copying facial expressions,
Language, empathy and social behavior.

These mirror neurons are the mechanism
That the brain utilizes to mimic.
Thus, we can learn the knowledge –
That has accumulated to our kind.

An organism with two percent of mass,
Consumes more than twenty percent of energy,
That is the brain's statistical impact.
The brain dominates our abilities.

In order to optimize energy usage,
The brain has windows of opportunity,
Where it is structured to mimic,
Each phase of knowledge that we need.

Process Relations
Cerebrum

It is really quite simple.
The mind is your tool to use.
It is formatted through the ages
And it is designed to function.

You must endeavor to harness
The power of the brain within.
The needs, the wants, the logic,
All to be harmonized in the process.

Each and everyone of us,
Endeavors to understand others.
We need to project their needs.
We need to understand motives.

This understanding of others
Is they key to "process relations".
The development of a strategy
Whereby agreement "to agree" is reached.

You are the possessor of your brain.
You should endeavor to exploit intellect.
This endeavor is a life long process:
Shaping our interactions with our world.

Real Mutations
RNA

The brain is not predestined.
It is ever alert and changing.
It processes information,
And builds on its environment.

The brain is in process of change.
It is altered by circumstance.
It is altered by learning.
It is altered by social inputs.

The very nature of one's self,
Is altered by the path we travel,
The ideas that we venture into.
The "self" is a unique individual.

The brain is the ultimate tool –
That we possess to form adaptation.
By adapting and altering processes,
We impose real mutations in the brain.

Libido
Striatum

The hormones surge forth within:
The imperative nature of lust,
The intensity is overriding,
Only intercourse fulfills the need.

This is the truth of nature:
Each and everyone feels the urge,
The hormones rule the body,
The mind is turned toward sex.

Testosterone controls the male.
Estriol dominates the female.
Don't explain "wait" and "later"!
It is now that needs release.

It is Called Love
(The Implanter)

A male in his early adulthood
Is a man loaded with testosterone
He is more aggressive and combative
Than at any time in his lifespan.

The male must demonstrate his prowess
To a female who will accept him to mate.
Without a mate, the male is evolutionarily voided:
No mate, no children, no immortality.

Men of old would combat 'til death
In order to become the implanter.
Women acknowledged the victor in turn,
Here is a man of strength with the victory.

Society has developed, the endeavor evolves.
Women seek strong, smart, aggressive mates.
Males must demonstrate prowess to mate;
In education, sports, business or war.

Killing a competitor is no longer civilized.
However, a handsome, intelligent and wealthy male
Is a desirable match for most females.
A prodigy produced in sexual harmony is the reward.

The Love Factory
Ventral Tegmenta –Nucleus Accumben –Caudate Nuclei

To meet, to get to know another;
And to begin the path to love.
It is normal in our species,
And necessary for our species.

The loving relationship begun with a kiss,
Can in due course lead to ecstasy.
Within the brain, dopamine rewards,
Creates cravings and passionate coupling.

As love develops and matures,
The brain is flooded with love's chemicals.
The dopamine activates "feel good" serotonin,
And finally the imprint binding chemical oxytocin.

The memory of love is indelibly inscribed
Within the brains repetitive habits knoll,
And early love gels into enduring commitment:
The essence of relations and child rearing.

This thing we call love is extraordinary.
It entices, rewards and binds us.
It takes place within our brains,
And is the super-glue of shared pairing.

The Brain House

Albert Einstein commented on brain usage,
"We use about ten percent of our brain
And that is when we are in overdrive."
Normally, he believed five percent the norm.

Brain scanning can identify usage.
The brain has multiple usage tie-ins.
A problem can activate many hot-spots.
The brain views problems dimensionally.

Only ten percent of the brain is lit-up
But locations are all over the brain.
Every part of the brain is being utilized.
A maximum effort is forthcoming.

At birth, the brain is not fully developed.
The birth canal is too small for a larger brain.
Babies must be natured to allow development.
This development continues into adult years.

The entire brain is being utilized.
Learning experiences and life's journey,
All contribute to our intellectual ability.
Each, battling for geography in the brain.

Brain Force

The brain is a dynamic circuit.
The essence of life is consciousness.
Flowing within the rivers of thought,
Is the process of daily adaptation.

Even in sleep, we sort, store and solve.
The shape of our thoughts change in the brain.
The evolution of man, and mankind,
Reside in this structure, we call brain.

We Begin With DNA

There are three generations of self.
The self which is the genetic mix
Of both your biological parents
And the self which comes from forebears.

These two dispositions plus your own,
This is the self you have as yourself,
Which adapts and develops to be you,
Which accumulates knowledge and experience.

This self can be alert and adapt,
Or it can be slow and inadaptable.
Each of us is a unique norm in time.
The norm changes as we change.

We pass our seed to a new generation.
Improvements in the gene pool are ongoing.
Those that do not improve are inferior,
Those with improvements are the pathfinders.

The gamble is always on the blending:
One male, one female, how to match?
This dilemma is solved by each individual.
No comprehensive combine is yet to be foolproof.

The New Brain

What do you mean, you are lost?
I'll turn on my GPS and locate,
You'll know within fifty yards
Where we are located right now.

You keep saying, you don't know.
My friend, google the question online.
You'll get hundreds of answers,
You just have to pick the one you like.

You cannot meet a girl you like.
You are really ignorant of life.
There are dating sites galore
With beautiful women all wanting you.

A flight, a vacation, a rental car,
All available online with one click.
You can get it all in one stop shopping.
Book it cheap, book it fast, book it now.

Whatever you want, whatever you need,
It is there for you on the internet:
Schooling, medical advice and financial advice.
Forget your brain, throw it away; google!

The Inner Universe
(Three Dimensions)

Scientists have opened a mystery within,
A window into the last unknown of man:
The inner workings of the brains circuitry,
Previously hidden behind gray fatty tissue.

Researchers have injected antibodies, targeting proteins,
The process allowed a three dimension viewing of all
The brains neurons, axons, dendrites and synapses.
This new universe within is now open to discovery.

All the brains interior, branches and connectivity
Will be studied, analyzed and defined with clarity.
The view will allow normal relative to abnormal,
Great brains relative to damaged or faulty brains.

The workings of the brain will unravel in time:
The very connections of life form and survival,
Of intellect and mankind's ability to achieve,
Of processes involved in our evolution.

The last frontier of human anatomy is on the horizon
As dawn begins within the dark recesses of the brain.
This "brain universe" will yield new discoveries
And illuminate the mind of man as never before.

Brain Reading 101

Looking into another's brain,
It is not as difficult as you think.
In reality, there are only seven choices.
One can guess which one's are in use.

Is it want or now, or both?
Is it fair or is it unfair?
Is he going to fight or flight?
Will he use judgment or logic?

Let us not forget trial and error,
The original brain learning system.
It is still in play today as we try,
First one method, and then another.

A checklist will do just fine.
You can watch a brain click thru,
As it filters from fair/unfair
To fight or maybe better flight.

The choices are limited and few.
It is one or another or a combine.
You can see if he wants it now,
Or will apply logic to problem solve.

This process is quite simple.
We all apply it in one form or another.
We try to read another's mind play,
Thus we can be ahead of the curve.

ADDENDUM
(Latin/English descriptive)

Straitum/WANTS
Limbic System/NOW
Anterior Insular/FAIR-UNFAIR
Nucleus Accumbens/TRIAL and ERROR
Amygdala/FIGHT or FLIGHT
Anterior Circulate/JUDGMENT/ARBITRATE
Prefrontal Cortex/LOGIC

Test Drive with your next conversation.
You will be surprised at the results.
You'll know if he is attentive,
Or have you lost his or her interest.

This skill set has many benefits.
Users can hone speaking skills,
Avoid conflict, close sales successfully,
And improve engagement with their audience.

ABOUT THE AUTHOR

John J. Duffy, the poet has published four poetry books and previously been nominated for the Pulitzer Prize in poetry. **Warman**, **Peaceman**, and **Sageman** document his war experience as a Special Forces Commander. His **The Bush Chronicles** gives a rendition of the most important events in George W. Bush's first term as President.

John served as a Commander in Special Operations and is a highly decorated officer. He rose from Sergeant to Major and has sixty plus awards and decoration including the Distinguished Service Cross and eight Purple Hearts.

After military service, John held senior positions in Publishing and Finance. He founded an investment firm which was sold to Ameritrade.

He is retired in Santa Cruz, California and writes poetry. Two of his poems are inscribed on a monument dedicated to Forward Air Controllers in Colorado Springs, Colorado.

John J. Duffy

Made in the USA
Charleston, SC
16 July 2013